Design: Jill Coote
Recipe Photography: Peter Barry
Jacket and Illustration Artwork: Jane Winton,
courtesy of Bernard Thornton Artists, London
Editors: Jillian Stewart, Kate Cranshaw and Laura Potts

CLB 3515

This edition published in 1994 by
Whitecap Books Ltd., 1086 West 3rd Street,
North Vancouver, B.C., Canada V7P 3JS
© 1994 CLB Publishing,
Godalming, Surrey, England.
Printed and bound in Singapore
Published 1994
ISBN 1-55110-203-X

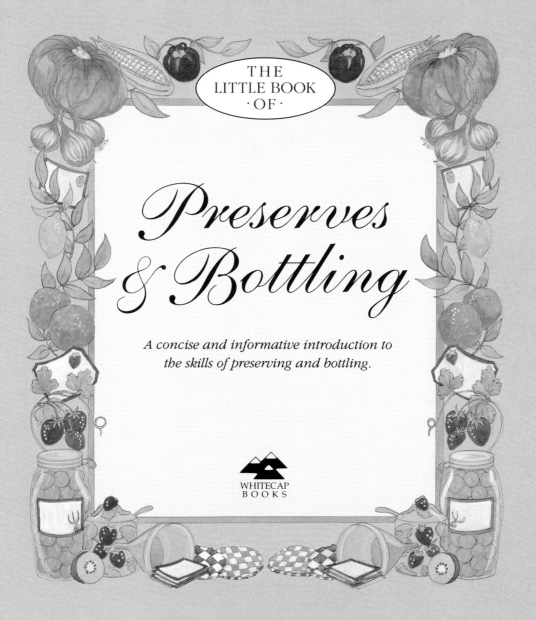

THE LITTLE BOOK ·OF·

Preserves & Bottling

A concise and informative introduction to the skills of preserving and bottling.

WHITECAP BOOKS

Introduction

The skills of preserving and bottling are fast becoming one of the forgotten arts of cookery, with people preferring the ease and convenience of buying the mass-produced, commercial product to making their own. Yet, when home-made preserves or pickles are available at a fair or swap meet, they are among the very first items to be sold, with people valuing their quality and flavor. Though making jams and pickles needs both time and patience, it is well worth the effort, with the finished result being far superior to commercial products. In addition, it is an ideal way of making use of the glut of inexpensive fruits and vegetables that are available in the summer and early fall.

Preserves can be divided roughly into three categories, jellies, jams, and marmalades. Jellies are made from the strained juice of pureed fruit, while jams are made from whole, cut, or pulped fruits, and marmalades from small, thin slices of fruit, usually citrus fruit. In each case the fruit is combined with sugar and water, and heated until the setting point is reached. Testing for this set can be done in a number of ways. The most popular is to spoon a small amount of the liquid onto a plate, where it should cool quickly and wrinkle when pushed with the finger.

Pectin, the substance that makes jams, jellies, and marmalades set, is vital to the process of making preserves. It is found naturally in fruits, with the greatest quantities occurring in the skin, seeds, and core. Some fruits contain much greater quantities of pectin than others, particularly apples, red and black currants, plums, and citrus fruits. In the past, small quantities of these fruits were used when making preserves with fruits that were low in pectin such as cherries, strawberries, raspberries, blackberries, and rhubarb, to ensure that they set. The development of commercial pectin has, save for the purposes of flavor, made this technique obsolete, giving far greater flexibility. Among the most popular forms in which to buy pectin, and probably the easiest to use, is sugar jam, which combines granulated sugar, and powdered pectin. It is important to follow recipes carefully as this minimizes the risk of problems in getting the preserve to set.

Pickling works on a slightly different principle to preserving. Preserves are made by using sugar to neutralize the effects of bacteria in fresh produce by dehydrating them, while pickles use acid, in most cases vinegar, to curtail the growth of unwanted bacteria, so stopping the food from going bad. When pickling, it is important to use produce that is at the very peak of condition and to prepare it carefully, as just one damaged vegetable can spoil the produce in a whole container.

The selection of recipes in this book provides the perfect introduction to the age-old skills of preserving and bottling, allowing you to discover the truly unique flavor of traditional, home-made preserves and pickles. With clear, step-by-step instructions and a host of useful tips, it guides you through some of the main techniques, as well as the principles underlying them, helping to get perfect results every time.

Whole Strawberry Conserve with Grand Marnier

MAKES About 12 cups

This luxury preserve will make an attractive gift for a gourmet. Make sure that you use only firm, unblemished berries.

PREPARATION: 10 mins
COOKING: 10 mins

8 cups strawberries
8 cups preserving sugar with added pectin or 8
    cups sugar and 2 tbsps pectin
4 tbsps lemon juice
4 tbsps Grand Marnier

1. Hull the strawberries, wash them, and leave to dry.

2. Layer the strawberries in a preserving pan, sprinkling the sugar between each layer.

3. Set aside until the juice begins to run.

4. Heat gently, stirring carefully until the sugar has dissolved. Add the lemon juice, then boil rapidly 5 minutes.

5. Remove from the heat and test to see if it has set. Some spooned onto a cold plate and left 2 minutes should wrinkle when tilted. If necessary boil a few more minutes.

6. Stir in the Grand Marnier. Allow the jam to cool considerably then stir to distribute the strawberries and pot into warm, sterilized jars. Seal and label.

Paradise Jelly

MAKES About 4 pounds

This jelly is made from a selection of tropical fruits. If passion fruits or granadilla are not available, use sapodilla or mamey.

PREPARATION: 15 mins
COOKING: 40 mins

2 small papayas (about 6 cups flesh)
4 passion fruits or granadilla
2 guavas
1½ cups canned crushed pineapple, in natural juice
⅓ cup water
2 tbsps lime juice
6 cups preserving sugar with added pectin or 6 cups sugar and 2 tbsps pectin

1. Peel and finely chop the papaya, and place in a preserving pan.

2. Cut the passion fruits or granadilla in half, scoop out pulp and seeds, then add to the pan.

3. Peel and chop the guavas and add to the pan.

4. Drain the pineapple and make juice up to 1 cup with water.

5. Add to the pan along with the pineapple.

6. Stir in the lime juice and cook gently until the fruit is very soft and pulpy.

7. Stir in the sugar, then heat gently, stirring until the sugar is dissolved.

8. Boil rapidly until setting point is reached. Some spooned onto a cold plate and left for 2 minutes should wrinkle when tilted.

9. Pour into hot, sterilized jelly jars, then seal and label.

Rhubarb and Raspberry Jam

MAKES About 9 cups

Raspberries can be expensive, but when mixed with rhubarb, just a few will produce a delicious fruity jam. Black or red raspberries or loganberries can be used.

PREPARATION: 30 mins
COOKING: 40 mins

3 cups rhubarb, cut into small pieces
⅔ cup water
6 cups raspberries
3 tbsps lemon juice
6 cups sugar

Cut the rhubarb into even-sized pieces about ½ inch long.

1. Place the rhubarb with the water, in a preserving pan and simmer gently 10 minutes or until the rhubarb is just soft.

2. Add the raspberries and lemon juice, and continue to cook 10 minutes or until all the fruit is very soft.

3. Stir in the sugar, and cook gently stirring until all the sugar has dissolved.

4. Boil rapidly until setting point is reached; some spooned onto a cold plate and left for 2 minutes should wrinkle when tilted.

5. Allow to stand 20 minutes then stir. Pour into hot, sterilized jars, seal and label.

Blueberry Jam with Cassis

MAKES About 8 cups

A sweet jam which can be made from fresh or frozen blueberries.

PREPARATION: 10 mins
COOKING: 35 mins

---

4 cups blueberries
1¼ cups water
3 tbsps lemon juice
4 cups sugar with added pectin or 4 cups sugar
    and 2 tbsps pectin
4 tbsps blackcurrant liqueur

---

1. Place the blueberries, water, and lemon juice in a preserving pan, and cook until the fruit is very soft.

2. Stir in the sugar and cook gently, stirring until all the sugar has dissolved.

3. Boil rapidly 5 minutes.

4. Remove from the heat and test for set; some spooned onto a cold plate and left for 2 minutes should wrinkle when tilted.

5. Boil for a little longer if required.

6. Stir in the blackcurrant liqueur.

7. Pour into hot, sterilized jars, then seal and label.

Lemon Lime Curd

MAKES About 3 cups
Delicious spread on bread or as a filling for cakes.

PREPARATION: 10 mins
COOKING: 50 mins

Grated rind and juice of 2 lemons
Grated rind and juice of 1 lime
3 tbsps unsalted butter
1 cup superfine sugar
3 eggs, beaten

1. Place the rind and juice of the fruit into the top of a double boiler or in a bowl placed over a pan of gently simmering water.

2. Add the butter and heat until melted. Stir in

Finely grate the rind of the lemons and lime.

Step 4 The curd is cooked when the mixture evenly coats the back of a wooden spoon.

the sugar and continue cooking until it has dissolved, stirring occasionally.

3. Strain the beaten eggs into the juice mixture and cook gently until the curd thickens, stirring constantly. Take care not to overheat the mixture or it will curdle. If the mixture does start to curdle, remove from the heat immediately and whisk rapidly.

4. The curd is cooked when the mixture coats the back of a spoon.

5. Pour into dry, sterilized jars, seal and label. Store in the refrigerator until required.

Kumquats in Cointreau

MAKES About 3 cups

Preserved whole fruits look and taste deliciously exotic. Serve with ice cream or as part of a fruit salad.

PREPARATION: 15-20 mins
COOKING: 45 mins-1 hr

---

5 cups whole kumquats
1 cup granulated sugar
2 cups water
3 tbsps Cointreau

---

1. Cut a cross in the top of each kumquat and pack into screwtop heatproof preserving jars.

2. Heat the sugar and water gently until the sugar dissolves, then boil 1 minute. Stir in the Cointreau.

3. Pour the syrup over the kumquats to within ⅓ inch of the top of the jar. Screw the lids onto

Step 1 Pack the kumquats into heatproof glass preserving jars.

the jars then release a quarter turn.

4. Place several layers of folded newspaper in the bottom of a pan which is deep enough to fill with water to the top of the jars. Place the jars in the pan.

5. Fill the pan with water, up to the necks of the jars and heat slowly to simmering point – this should take about 30 minutes.

6. Maintain the water at simmering point 10 minutes or until the kumquats look clear.

7. Remove the jars from the water and place on a wooden surface. Immediately fully tighten the lids and allow to cool completely.

8. Label and store in a cool, dark place.

Step 1 Cut a small cross in the rounded end of each kumquat.

Ginger Pear Jam

MAKES About 5 pints

Often a glut of pears leaves you wondering how you can use them up. This recipe is an ideal way, allowing you to savor the taste of fresh pears right through the winter.

PREPARATION: 20 mins
COOKING: 50 mins

4 pounds firm pears
3¾ cups water
4 tbsps grated fresh root ginger
Juice of 1 lemon
6 cups granulated sugar

1. Peel and core the pears, and cut them into thick slices. Place in a preserving pan with the water, ginger, and lemon juice.

Step 1 Cut the pears into thick slices with a sharp knife.

Step 2 Tie the peel, core, and lemon skins in a square of cheesecloth.

2. Tie the peel and core in a square of cheesecloth, and add to the pan. Cook the pears about 30 minutes, or until soft and pulpy.

3. Remove the cheesecloth bag. Mash the fruit or push through a sieve.

4. Stir in the sugar and heat gently, stirring until it is dissolved.

5. Boil rapidly until the setting point is reached. This should take about 20 minutes. Draw a wooden spoon through the mixture, if the spoon leaves a channel, setting point has been reached.

6. Pour into hot, sterilized jars, seal and label.

Kiwi Fruit and Apple Honey

MAKES About 5 cups

A refreshing and interesting preserve that spreads like honey.

PREPARATION: 15 mins
COOKING: 50 mins

---

4 kiwi fruits
⅔ cup water
2 cups sugar
2 cups honey
2 cups sharp apples, peeled, cored and finely
    chopped
1 tsp lemon juice
Green food coloring (optional)

---

1. Peel and chop the kiwi fruits.

2. Heat the water, sugar, and honey together in a preserving pan, stirring until all the sugar dissolves.

3. Add the kiwi fruits, apple, and lemon juice and cook very gently until the preserve darkens and thickens.

4. Stir frequently to prevent the jam from burning.

5. Allow the jam to cool slightly, then place in a food processor and blend until smooth, adding a little green food coloring, if wished.

6. Leave to stand a few minutes to allow the bubbles to disperse, then pour into hot, sterilized jars. Seal and label.

Pineapple Grapefruit Marmalade

MAKES About 5 pounds/3 quarts

The flavors of pineapple and grapefruit complement each other wonderfully as demonstrated in this delicious and unusual recipe.

PREPARATION: 1 hr
COOKING: 1½ hrs

---

2 large pineapples
3 grapefruits
2½ cups water
3 cups granulated sugar
1 tbsp butter (if necessary)

---

1. Peel and cut the pineapples into small pieces.

2. Wash the grapefruits and pare off the zest with a sharp knife, taking care to include as little as possible of the white part.

3. Cut the peel into shreds and squeeze the juice from the fruit.

4. Tie the remaining white parts and seeds in a square of cheesecloth.

Step 1 Peel the pineapple with a sharp knife.

Step 3 Cut the grapefruit peel into fine shreds.

5. Put the juice, peel, cheesecloth bag, and pineapple into a preserving pan with the water. Simmer gently about 1 hour, or until the peel is soft.

6. Remove the cheesecloth bag and squeeze out well. Stir the sugar into the pan and heat gently, stirring until all the sugar is dissolved.

7. Boil rapidly without stirring until the setting point is reached. Spoon some marmalade onto a cold plate and leave for 2 minutes. It should wrinkle when tilted.

8. If the marmalade looks bubbly and cloudy, stir the butter through the mixture to help clear it.

9. Allow to stand 20 minutes before bottling. Pour into hot, sterilized jars, seal, and label.

Three Fruit Marmalade

MAKES About 7 cups

This marmalade can be made at any time of the year, unlike those which include Seville (bitter) oranges in the ingredients, which can only be made in winter.

PREPARATION: 45 mins
COOKING: 1½ hrs

4 limes
2 oranges
2 grapefruits
5 cups water
4 cups granulated sugar
2 tbsps butter (if necessary)

Step 2 Shred the citrus fruit zest into very thin strips.

1. Wash the fruits and pare off the zest with a sharp knife, taking care not to include too much of the white part.

2. Cut the zest into shreds and squeeze the juice from the fruit.

3. Tie the remaining white part and seeds in a square of cheesecloth.

4. Put the juice, peel, and cheesecloth bag into a preserving pan with the water and simmer gently for about 1 hour, or until the peel is soft and the contents of the pan have been reduced by about half.

5. Remove the cheesecloth bag, and squeeze out well. Stir in the sugar and heat gently, stirring until all the sugar has dissolved.

6. Boil rapidly without stirring until setting point is reached. Some spooned onto a cold plate and left for 2 minutes should wrinkle when tilted.

7. If the marmalade looks bubbly and cloudy, stir the butter through the mixture to help clear it.

8. Allow to stand 20 minutes before potting. Pour into hot, sterilized jars, seal, and label.

Plums in Port Wine

MAKES About 4 pounds/5 pints
This makes a very sophisticated dessert.

PREPARATION: 40 mins
COOKING: 40 mins

⅔ cup water
1 cup sugar
1¼ cups ruby port
6 cups plums, halved and pitted
Few whole cloves

---

1. Heat the water and sugar, gently stirring until the sugar dissolves, then boil for a few minutes.

2. Remove from the heat and stir in the port.

3. Pack the plums into heatproof preserving jars, and add 1 or 2 cloves to each jar.

4. Pour in the sirup to within ⅓ inch of the top of the jars. Add a little extra port if there is not enough sirup.

5. Screw down the lids then release a quarter turn.

6. Place several layers of folded newspaper in the bottom of a deep pan.

7. Put the jars in, and fill the pan with water to the necks.

8. Heat slowly to simmering – this should take 30 minutes. Simmer 10 minutes.

9. Turn off the heat, tighten the lids, and allow the jars to cool completely in the water.

10. Label and store in a cool, dark place.

Pineapple, Mango, and Mint Chutney

MAKES About 3 pounds/6 cups

This fresh-tasting, sweet pickle makes an ideal accompaniment for snack lunches and picnic meals.

PREPARATION: 20 mins
COOKING: 35 mins

---

1 large pineapple
Salt
2 large mangoes, peeled, stoned, and chopped
1 cup yellow raisins
3¾ cups white vinegar (acetic acid)
3 tbsps chopped fresh mint
1 tbsp chopped fresh root ginger
½ tsp ground nutmeg
4 cups granulated sugar

---

1. Peel the pineapple and chop the flesh. Layer in a shallow dish, sprinkle liberally with salt, and leave for several hours, or overnight.

2. Rinse the pineapple and drain well.

3. Place the pineapple, mango, yellow raisins, vinegar, mint, ginger, and nutmeg in a preserving pan and simmer gently for 10 minutes, or until the fruits are tender.

4. Stir in the sugar and heat gently until it dissolves, then boil rapidly until thickened, stirring frequently to prevent it from sticking to the bottom of the pan and burning.

5. Test by stirring with a wooden spoon – if the spoon leaves a channel then the mixture is ready.

6. Pour into hot, sterilized jars, seal, and label.

Curried Fruits

MAKES About 5 cups

This pickle is very quick to make and goes particularly well with cold pork.

PREPARATION: 15 mins
COOKING: 15 mins

---

1 cup raw cane sugar
⅔ cup malt vinegar
5 fl oz water
4 whole cloves
2 tbsps mild curry powder
1 tsp coriander seeds
3 apples, peeled, cored, and thickly sliced
¾ cup diced pineapple
½ cup raisins
6 apricots, pitted and halved

---

1. Place the sugar, vinegar, water, cloves, curry powder, and coriander seeds in a large saucepan or preserving pan.

2. Heat gently, stirring until the sugar dissolves, then boil 2 minutes.

3. Add the apples, pineapple, and raisins and cook 5 minutes.

4. Add the apricots and cook another 3 minutes. The apple should look translucent.

5. Pour into hot, sterilized jars, then seal and label.

6. Once opened, store in the refrigerator.

Bread-and-Butter Pickle

MAKES About 5 cups

A simple, attractive pickle. Serve with fish or cold meats.

PREPARATION: 15 mins, plus several hours standing time
COOKING: 10 mins

1¼ pounds small pickling cucumbers
1 large onion
Salt
2½ cups malt vinegar
4 cups sugar
2 tbsps mustard seeds
½ tsp turmeric
1 tsp celery seeds
Pinch cayenne pepper

---

1. Slice the cucumbers and onion very thinly and place in a shallow dish.

2. Sprinkle liberally with salt, cover with a weighted lid, and leave for at least 6 hours. Drain, rinse well in cold water, and drain again.

3. Place the remaining ingredients in a large pan and bring to the boil, stirring well.

4. Boil 2-3 minutes, and add the sliced cucumber, and onion.

5. Boil for 5 minutes or until the cucumber looks translucent.

6. Pour into hot, sterilized jars, then seal with acid-proof lids, and label. Store in the refrigerator.

Corn Relish

MAKES About 4 cups

Popular for barbecues, this relish is delicious on sausages and hamburgers.

PREPARATION: 20 mins
COOKING: 35 mins

⅔ cup chopped celery
1 onion, chopped
2 tsps celery seasoning
1 tsp mustard seed
¼ tsp turmeric
1 tbsp cornstarch
½ cups vinegar
1 cup water
1½ cups corn niblets, fresh or frozen
2 red bell peppers, diced
½ cup sugar

---

1. Place the celery, onion, celery seasoning, mustard seeds, turmeric, and cornstarch in a large saucepan.

2. Gradually stir in the vinegar and water. Bring gently to the boil, stirring constantly, and cook 5 minutes.

3. Stir in the corn, diced peppers, and sugar and cook slowly for 25 minutes, stirring occasionally, until the mixture is very thick and the vegetables are tender. When a wooden spoon is drawn through the mixture it should leave a channel.

4. Pour into hot, sterilized jars, then seal and label.

Piccalilli

MAKES About 3 pounds (6 cups)

A British mustard pickle based on an Indian recipe. Any vegetables can be used, but this combination works well.

PREPARATION: 20 mins, plus 6 hrs standing
COOKING: 15-20 mins

1½ cups diced pickling cucumbers
1½ cups chopped onions
1½ cups cauliflower, cut into small flowerets
1 large green bell pepper, diced
Salt
1¼ cups vinegar
2 tbsps French mustard
½ tsp turmeric
½ tsp mustard seeds
¼ tsp dried thyme
1 bayleaf
60g/2oz sugar
1 tbsp cornstarch mixed with a little water

---

1. Layer the vegetables in a dish, sprinkle each layer liberally with salt.

2. Leave for at least 6 hours to draw out water from the vegetables. Rinse and drain well.

3. Place the vegetables in a large saucepan or preserving pan and add the vinegar, mustard, turmeric, mustard seeds, thyme, bayleaf, and sugar.

4. Stir to mix well. Bring gently to the boil and simmer 8 minutes, or until the vegetables are cooked but still crisp.

5. Stir in the cornstarch mixture and cook until thickened.

6. Pour into hot, sterilized jars, then seal with acid-proof lids, and label. Store refrigerated.

Sweet Pickled Onions

MAKES About 8 cups

Nothing can compare with the flavor of home-made pickled onions, perfect for picnics, salads, or with bread and cheese.

PREPARATION: 20 mins
COOKING: 1 hr

3 pounds button or pearl onions
3¾ cups wine or cider vinegar
1½ cups light brown sugar
2 tbsps mustard seeds
1 cinnamon stick
1 tsp salt

1. Pour boiling water over the onions to loosen the skins, then peel them.

2. Bring a large pan of water to the boil, add a couple of tablespoons of the vinegar, add the onions and blanch 5 minutes.

3. Drain the onions and pat dry, then pack tightly into heatproof preserving jars.

Step 1 Drain the blanched onions and peel the skins.

Step 4 Pour the boiling vinegar over the onions to within ⅓ inch of the top of the jar.

4. Heat the remaining ingredients together until boiling and pour over the onions to within ⅓ inch of the top of the jar. Screw the lids onto the jars then release a quarter turn.

5. Place several layers of folded newspaper in the bottom of a heavy-based pan which is deep enough to fill with water to the top of the jars. Place the jars in the pan.

6. Fill the pan with water up to the neck of the jars and heat slowly to simmering point; this should take about 30 minutes.

7. Maintain the water at simmering point for 10 minutes.

8. Turn off the heat, tighten the lids, and allow the jars to cool completely in the water.

9. Label and store in a cool dark place.

Pumpkin Chutney

MAKES About 8 cups

A chunky pickle, delicious served with a salad or a snack lunch.

PREPARATION: 20 mins
COOKING: 45 mins

---

6 cups pumpkin flesh, small diced
2 lemons, thinly sliced
2 tbsps grated fresh root ginger
1½ cups raisins
3 cups water
2¼ cups white wine vinegar
4 cups light brown sugar

---

1. Place all the ingredients except the sugar in a preserving pan. Cook gently 20-30 minutes until the pumpkin is tender.

2. Stir in the sugar and heat gently until it is dissolved.

3. Increase the heat and bring to the boil. Boil rapidly until thickened, stirring frequently to prevent it from sticking to the bottom of the pan and burning.

4. Test by stirring with a wooden spoon; if the spoon leaves a channel then the mixture is ready.

5. Pour into hot, sterilized jars, then seal and label.

Index

Kumquats in Cointreau – delicious served with ice cream.